Tasty Homemade Waffle Recipes Cookbook

Lenny .Y Thorpe

Tasty Homemade Waffle Recipes Cookbook : Delicious Waffle Recipes for Breakfast and Brunch Made at Home

Funny helpful tips:

Stay diligent; consistent effort often yields the best results.

Stay connected with industry peers; collaborations can offer mutual benefits.

Life advices:

Stay hopeful; optimism is a beacon in challenging times.

Seek mutual respect; it's the cornerstone of a healthy relationship.

Introduction

Welcome to the world of culinary creativity with this book. Within these pages, you'll discover the wonders of the mini waffle maker—a compact yet mighty kitchen gadget that opens up a world of delicious possibilities. From savory omelets to classic waffle creations and decadent desserts, this cookbook celebrates the versatility and ingenuity of the mini waffle maker.

As you journey through the pages of this cookbook, you'll learn that size truly doesn't matter when it comes to flavor and creativity in the kitchen. Despite its diminutive stature, the mini waffle maker proves to be a culinary powerhouse, capable of producing an array of mouthwatering dishes that are sure to impress even the most discerning palates.

With its user-friendly design and intuitive operation, the mini waffle maker makes cooking a breeze, allowing you to whip up delicious meals with ease. Whether you're a seasoned chef or a novice cook, mastering the art of waffle making has never been simpler.

One of the joys of cooking with the mini waffle maker is the freedom to let your imagination run wild. Experiment with different ingredients, flavors, and textures to create unique dishes that reflect your personal taste and style. From cheesy omelets to indulgent desserts, the possibilities are endless.

Cleanup is a breeze with the mini waffle maker, thanks to its non-stick surface and compact design. Say goodbye to scrubbing stubborn residue and hello to effortless cleanup, allowing you to spend less time washing dishes and more time enjoying your culinary creations.

The mini waffle maker's compact size and portability make it the perfect addition to any kitchen, no matter how small or crowded. With its sleek design and space-saving features, you'll never have to worry about finding a place to store your mini waffle maker again.

Unlock the full potential of your mini waffle maker with insider tips and expert guidance from the chef. Whether you're perfecting your batter consistency or mastering the art of flipping, these tips will help you take your waffle-making game to the next level.

Finally, dive into an array of mouthwatering recipes that showcase the versatility and creativity of the mini waffle maker. From savory classics to sweet treats, there's something for everyone to enjoy. With this book as your guide, you'll be well on your way to becoming a waffle-making aficionado.

Contents

The Amazing Mini Waffle Maker

The Amazing Mini Waffle Maker is the next new innovative kitchen gadget that would fit perfectly in your kitchen or as a gift for a friend of family. Just imagine sitting down to a perfect brunch with the family over personal sized waffles made just for them. You can create these in your amazing mini waffle maker and much more.!

This waffle maker not only makes delicious waffles, but can whip up anything from omelets and tacos, to burgers, steak and desserts. Just think of all of the things that you can do with this product that have nothing to do with a traditional waffle. Why wouldn't you want to have one of these in your kitchen?

The Amazing Mini Waffle Maker not only allows you to be creative but is so small that it can fit directly in your purse, handbag, or backpack for easy travel. Now, you can take this device anywhere and make up some delicious waffles or recipes at your friend's next dinner party. This way you can share the wealth with your family and your friends no matter where you are. We guarantee they will fall in love with it as well. And, they will be asking you to use it at the next dinner party that you are hosting at your place.

This cookbook was put together to help you create wonderful recipes in a new and innovative way. So, why are you still standing there? Flip the page and let's get started!

Just Waffle It!

For those of us who are waffle loves, the idea of making anything into a waffle just drives us crazy. Have you ever looked at your waffle maker and wondered what else you could make in it? Well, this cookbook will answer all of those questions for you.

Let's just say that you can cook almost anything in the mini waffle maker. This cookbook provides recipes for omelets and other breakfast dishes, to meat, sandwiches, burgers, comfort food and desserts.

Everything you make in the mini waffle maker has the same Belgian waffle look and crispiness. Your children will love making things from grilled cheese, to spaghetti and meatballs with a waffle feel and look. Who wouldn't want that?

Take the kids into the kitchen and have them help you. Waffle days and nights can be fun for the whole family.

Does Size Really Matter???

Most waffle makers are big and bulky. Not the mini waffle maker! The mini waffle maker was made small for a couple of different reasons. First, it is travel size and can fit in your purse or backpack for easy travel and access. It doesn't take up much counter space and can be tucked away in your cupboard without having to find a ton of storage space for it.

The second reason that the mini waffle maker was created, and the most important, is the fact that you can personalize each time you put pour your batter or other ingredients in it. If someone you know is allergic or doesn't like a particular ingredient, you can make a personalized dish that is catered to their individualized needs or tastes without all of the hassle. This way everyone is happy and gets what they want without complaint. And, it makes that person feel special as well.

It is a win-win in everyone's book and ours too!

Cheese That We Found Best for Omelet Waffles

I would have to say that cheese is one of the most used ingredient in an omelet besides using eggs of course. Cheese in an omelet is nice and gooey and will help to hold the omelet together giving an assorted range of flavors depending on the types of cheese you use.

Below are some cheeses that we thought you would love and enjoy and can substitute with any of the recipes that we have in this book.

Boursin Cheese

This is a soft creamy cheese available in a variety of flavors, with a flavor and texture somewhat similar to cream cheese. The first Boursin flavor, Garlic and Fine Herbs, was created in 1957 by François Boursin, a cheese maker from Normandy.

Cheddar Cheese

It is buttery and milky tasting, it has a natural gray rind and creamy beige-to-yellow interior. Mild and salty it is one of the most easily digested cheeses. Cantal is also known as Cantal de Salers and is a French Cheese. Less dense than Cheddar, it's flavor is more refined.

Chèvre Cheese

This word is French for Goat's cheese that is made out of goat's milk. A majority of goat cheeses come from France.

Cream Cheese

The cheese has a mildly lactic aroma and a slightly salty taste. The taste, texture and production are similar to Boursin and Mascarpone. Cream cheese is suitable for vegetarians since it uses acid, such as citric acid to coagulate the milk. Cream cheese has a mild, sweet taste with a pleasant slight tang.

Feta Cheese

On the whole, Feta is a pickled curd cheese that has a salty and tangy taste enhanced by the brine solution. The texture depends on the age which can be extremely creamy, or crumbly dry. It delicious in taste with nuts roasted red peppers and olive oil.

Fontina Cheese

Normally mild in taste, this cheese melts easily thanks to its firm and slightly grainy texture. For use in fondue, Gruyère produces a rich and creamy sauce similar to that of Fontina. Sharp and with a touch of hazelnut and butter, this cheese sits well with a wide variety of different meats and vegetables.

Gouda Cheese

It is characterized by its nutty and sweet flavor, and its dense texture. Made from cow's milk, the flavors and aromas sharpen as it ages. A closer look at the Gouda flavor, Cheddar offers a similar density and texture.

Gruyère Cheese

This cheese is a little sweet but slightly salty, with a flavor that varies widely with age. It is often described as creamy and nutty when young, becoming more assertive, earthy, and complex as it matures. When fully aged (five months to a year) it tends to have small cracks that impart a slightly grainy texture.

Mozzarella Cheese

This cheese has a soft, moist texture and is full of milky flavor. Similar to other fresh cheeses, mozzarella fresco is high in water content and therefore low on fat. It has a slightly acidic or lactic taste. Compared to mass-processed mozzarellas, the freshly made variant is creamier and much softer.

Parmesan Cheese

The product is aged an average of two years. The cheese is produced daily, and it can show a natural variability. True Parmigiano-Reggiano cheese has a sharp, complex fruity/nutty taste with a strong savory flavor and a slightly gritty texture. Inferior versions can impart a bitter taste.

Pimiento Cheese

They come in both sweet and hot varieties. Pimentos are commonly used raw and sliced in salads. The name "pimento" comes from the Portuguese word for bell pepper. The flavor of a pimento is similar to that of a bell pepper, but its taste is more tangy and pungent.

Ricotta Cheese

Ricotta is a smooth cheese with a creamy mild taste and a thick texture. Its light flavor and low salt content make it perfect for using in sweet or savory dishes. It can also be air-cured or dried in the oven to make it into a harder, sharp-tasting cheese that can be grated.

A Little Waffle History...101!

Waffle-making made its way to America with Dutch colonists in the 1620s. It was one hundred years later, in Robert Smith's *Court Cookery* , that the English language saw the appearance of the word "waffle" for the first time. Waffles were enjoyed sweet, with butter, syrup, or fruit, or savory, with kidney stew.

While the waffle iron can be traced all the way back to ancient Greece, the earliest irons in the museum's Domestic Life collection date to the early 18th century and take the form of two hinged plates at the end of long handles called reins. The waffle iron below was used by a family in Morgantown, West Virginia, between 1810 and 1850 and features a ring of squares surrounding a central rosette. With the introduction of the wood stove, the handles of waffle irons were shortened to be used over the cooktop rather than in an open hearth.

Simple to Use

The mini waffle maker is easy and simple to use!

Safeguards

- ☐ The cooking surface and cover of the device is extremely hot when in use. It is important that you never touch the cover of cooking surface when cooking.
- ☐ When lifting the cover, do not open with your arm directly over the surface of the device. The heat may cause injury.
- ☐ Make sure to open and close the cover by using the cover handle. Remember to lift from the side.

How to use

- ☐ Set the mini waffle maker on a hard and dry surface. Plug the cord in and the light on the cover will light up indicating that the mini waffle maker is warming up.
- ☐ The light on the cover of the mini waffle maker will shut off automatically when it reaches the temperature it needs to start cooking.
- ☐ Lift the cover using the handle and spray both sides with cooking spray.
- ☐ Pour the batter or ingredients in the mini waffle maker and close the cover.
- ☐ Once the ingredients are done cooking, remove it from the mini waffle maker with a utensil that is not metal.
- ☐ When you are done cooking, unplug the mini waffle maker and allow it to cool down before cleaning or storing.

Be as Creative as You Can Be

The great thing about this new and innovative product is that you can be as creative as you want. We have provided quite a few recipes within this book to help provide a framework that will help get your creative juices flowing.

Believe me when we started exploring, we started to see what the mini waffle maker can do. We stepped into our test kitchen and started throwing together ingredients that we knew and loved, and that others would like to try in their mini waffle maker as well.

With this being said, step into your kitchen laboratory and start mixing together some of the ingredients that you would love to see made in the mini waffle maker, and then send us a review and tell us how the recipe turned out. We would love to hear back from you.

Food We've Tried, that Aren't Waffles

Waffled Eggs
Waffled Hash Browns
Waffled Tomatoes
Waffled Cake

The great thing about this new and innovative product is that you can be as creative as you want. We have provided quite a few recipes within this book to help provide a framework that will help get your creative juices flowing.

However, just because it is not a waffle doesn't mean that it can't be cooked in a mini waffle maker.

Here are some other items we've tried that worked in the mini waffle maker that we used:

1. Shredded Yams
2. Hash Browns
3. Fried Eggs
4. Cooked Top Ramen
5. Cooked Rice

These are just a few items that will get the juices flowing. Try some of your own. You'll be surprised at what you can waffle!

Cleaning is a Breeze

Here are some helpful cleaning and maintenance instructions.

- ☐ Allow the mini waffle maker to cool off completely before you do anything.
- ☐ NEVER submerge the mini waffle maker in water or any other type of liquid.
- ☐ NEVER use any abrasive cleaning agents or liquids because they can damage the mini waffle maker.
- ☐ It is imperative to clean your mini waffle maker after each use to prevent from oils or food to build up in it.
- ☐ Use a clean, damp, and soapy cloth to wipe down the inside and outside of the mini waffle maker. Rinse the cloth and repeat as needed.
- ☐ Make sure it is dry before you store it.
- ☐ If there is any food that is burnt on the surface, you can clean it off with some cooking oil. Pour the cooking oil on it and let it sit for 5-10 minutes. Then scrub with a sponge or

soft bristled brush to get off any food that is stuck. Then use a damp, soapy cloth to wipe down again, and repeat if needed.

☐   If the food still remains, let the cooking oil sit for a few hours and then wipe down.

Store it Anywhere

The mini waffle maker is mini for a reason! It is travel size and is easy to store.

Often times appliances take up a lot of space in your cupboards and have instructions on where they can be stored and what appliances can be stored next to them or on top of them.

This is not the case with the mini waffle maker. It can be stored anywhere without ruining its non-stick surface. It is also so small that it doesn't take up a lot of space. This way you don't have to move a lot of things around to make room for it.

What other proof do you need to use this amazing product and buy one for every single friend and member of your family?

Pro Tips from the Chef

1. *Adding a little corn starch:*

This is a trick that will add a little more crispness to your waffles. You have to try it to believe it!

2. Air Fryer or Toaster Oven for even more crisp waffles:

After your waffles are done there is usually time for them to sit and cook. We took ours and pre-heated an air fryer on 350 for 3-4 min. This adds an extra texture that only you will know when you do this!

3. Buttermilk for a boost in taste:

This will make a world of difference to your waffles and you will see the difference. It will give a little better quality of flavor.

4. Use a waffle maker that can flip:

These machines always cook waffles more evenly because after the batter is poured in, it gets flipped. Then the batter can spread evenly making the perfect waffles.

5. Add a nice liqueur for succulent taste:

This is for sure a pro tip that will leave you speechless!!! When others do this, they leave out the vanilla, however, I keep the vanilla and add the liqueur (amaretto, Malibu run, etc.)

Omelettes

Onion & Cheese Omelet Mini Waffle

Try this new waffle with a twist. This recipe is paired with eggs and vegetables for a crispier version on this classic.

Prep Time: 5 Minutes
Cook Time: 5 Minutes
Servings: 1

Ingredients

2 eggs
1 Orange bell pepper
1 Tomato
1 Red onion
2 tbsp. milk
Salt to taste
Pepper to taste
Cheese, for topping

Directions

Wash and dice vegetables.
Crack eggs and mix in a bowl with salt and pepper along with the veggies.
Pour 2 tbsps. milk to the eggs and whisk.
Spray the waffle maker with oil. Pour 2 tbsps. batter into waffle maker and cook until crispy. Repeat until all batter is used.
Serve with shredded cheese if desired.

Cheesy Jalapeño Mini Waffle Omelet

For those who like it a little, Hot-n-Spicy! This Wyoming recipe is a great jump start to make sure you get your day started the right way. Guaranteed to wake you up!.

Prep Time: 5 Minutes
Cook Time: 5 Minutes
Servings: 1

Ingredients

2 eggs
1 Jalapeño
1 sweet onion
2 tbsp. milk
Salt to taste
Pepper to taste
Cheddar Cheese, for topping (shredded)

Directions

Wash and dice vegetables.
Crack eggs and mix in a bowl with salt and pepper, along with the diced vegetables.
Pour 2 tbsps. milk to the eggs and whisk.
Spray the waffle maker with oil. Pour 2 tbsps. batter into waffle maker and cook until crispy. Repeat until all batter is used.
Serve with shredded cheese if desired.

Super Spinach Mini Waffle Omelet

Just like mom used to tell you… "Eat your greens!" This is exactly what we did with this green machine delight. A healthier style omelet!

Prep Time: 5 Minutes
Cook Time: 5 Minutes
Servings: 1

Ingredients

2 eggs
1 cup spinach diced
1 sweet onion
2 tbsp. milk
Salt to taste
Pepper to taste
Cheddar Cheese, for topping (shredded)

Directions

Wash and dice vegetables.
Crack eggs and mix in a bowl with salt and pepper, along with the diced vegetables.
Pour 2 tbsps. milk to the eggs and whisk.
Spray the waffle maker with oil. Pour 2 tbsps. batter into waffle maker and cook until crispy. Repeat until all batter is used.
Serve with shredded cheese and more tomatoes if desired.

Super Jalapeño Spinach Mini Waffle Omelet

Kick up the heat on the omelet. Perfect for those looking to turn up the heat. Amazing flavor on this amazing delight.

Prep Time: 5 Minutes
Cook Time: 5 Minutes
Servings: 1

Ingredients

2 eggs
1 cup jalapeño diced
1 cup spinach diced
1 sweet onion
2 tbsp. milk
Salt to taste
Pepper to taste
Cheddar Cheese, for topping (shredded)

Directions

Wash and dice vegetables.
Crack eggs and mix in a bowl with salt and pepper, along with the diced vegetables.
Pour 2 tbsps. milk to the eggs and whisk.
Spray the waffle maker with oil. Pour 2 tbsps. batter into waffle maker and cook until crispy. Repeat until all batter is used.
Serve with shredded cheese and more tomatoes if desired.

Jalapeño Blueberry Mini Waffle Omelet

You never thought these two went together. The heat from the jalapeños and the sweet rich taste of the blueberries makes for something wonderful.

Prep Time: 5 Minutes
Cook Time: 5 Minutes
Servings: 1

Ingredients
2 eggs
1 cup jalapeño diced
1 cup spinach diced
1 sweet onion
2 tbsp. milk
Salt to taste
Pepper to taste
Cheddar Cheese, for topping (shredded)

Directions
Wash and dice vegetables.
Crack eggs and mix in a bowl with salt and pepper, along with the diced vegetables.
Pour 2 tbsps. milk to the eggs and whisk.
Spray the waffle maker with oil. Pour 2 tbsps. batter into waffle maker and cook until crispy. Repeat until all batter is used.
Serve with shredded cheese and more tomatoes if desired.

Cheesy Parmesan Ham Sandwich Mini Waffle Omelet

We can make a sandwich out of anything, but this delicious dish will be something to brag about after you serve it to a friend or someone special.

Prep Time: 5 Minutes
Cook Time: 5 Minutes
Servings: 1

Ingredients

2 eggs
2 slices of ham (per sandwich)
½ tsp. Paprika
1 sweet onion
2 tbsp. milk
Salt to taste
Pepper to taste
Parmesan, for topping (shredded)

Directions

Wash and dice vegetables.
Crack eggs and mix in a bowl with salt and pepper, along with the diced vegetables.
Pour 2 tbsps. milk to the eggs and whisk.
Spray the waffle maker with oil. Pour 2 tbsps. batter into waffle maker and cook until crispy. Repeat until you get a top and bottom omelet.
Put the parmesan cheese on one of the omelets.
Then add the 2 pieces of ham. If the ham hangs over then you can fold it.

The cheese should be melted and all good to eat.
For more sandwiches, repeat until all batter is used.
Taste great with tobacco sauce or Sriracha sauce.

Greek Mediterranean Mini Waffle Omelet Sandwich

We can make a sandwich out of anything, but this delicious dish will be something to brag about after you serve it to a friend or someone special.

Prep Time: 5 Minutes
Cook Time: 5 Minutes
Servings: 1

Ingredients
2 eggs
5 sliced Greek Olives
½ tsp. Paprika
½ red onion
2 tbsp. milk
Salt to taste
Pepper to taste
Feta cheese, for topping (shredded)

Directions
Wash and dice vegetables.
Crack eggs and mix in a bowl with salt and pepper, along with the diced vegetables.
Pour 2 tbsps. milk to the eggs and whisk.
Spray the waffle maker with oil. Pour 2 tbsps. batter into waffle maker and cook until crispy. Repeat until you get a top and bottom omelet.
Crumble the Feta cheese on one of the omelets along with ½ of the Greek olives. Then put the 2nd omelet on top of that and crumble more Feta cheese on top.

For more sandwiches, repeat until all batter is used.
Taste great with tzatziki sauce.

Big Meat Cheddar Mini Waffle Omelet

Some things were just made to be meaty. If you like meat in your omelets then this will be a true winner for you!

Prep Time: 5 Minutes
Cook Time: 5 Minutes
Servings: 1

Ingredients

2 eggs
1 red bell pepper
¼ lb. cooked bacon
¼ lb. cooked ground beef
2 slices of ham chopped
2 tbsp. milk
Salt to taste
Pepper to taste
Cheddar cheese, for topping

Directions

Wash and dice vegetables.
Crack eggs and mix in a bowl with salt and pepper, vegetables and meats.
Pour 2 tbsps. milk to the eggs and whisk.
Spray the waffle maker with oil. Pour 2 tbsps. batter into waffle maker and cook until crispy. Repeat until all batter is used.
Serve with shredded cheddar. Goes great with ketchup or hot sauce.

Californian Mini Waffle Omelet

Eat your heart out for this special delight! Straight from the heart of Southern California, where we discovered this omelet. Great source of healthy fats!

Prep Time: 5 Minutes
Cook Time: 5 Minutes
Servings: 1

Ingredients

2 eggs
1 avocado (sliced)
1 sweet onion (chopped)
2 tbsp. milk
Salt to taste
Pepper to taste
Cheddar Cheese, for topping (shredded)

Directions

Wash and dice vegetables.
Crack eggs and mix in a bowl with salt and pepper, along with the sweet onions.
Pour 2 tbsps. milk to the eggs and whisk.
Spray the waffle maker with oil. Pour 2 tbsps. batter into waffle maker and cook until crispy. Repeat until all batter is used.
Atop the waffle omelets with the avocado! When waffles are warm the avocado will spread easily!
Serve with shredded cheese sprinkled on top if desired.

Texas Rib Eye Mini Waffle Omelet

We bring you the great taste of Texas to this waffle omelet. So, steak is on the menu! This great delight is for those who enjoy a nice and hearty meal!

Prep Time: 5 Minutes
Cook Time: 5 Minutes
Servings: 1

Ingredients

2 eggs
½ lb steak of your choice (we prefer Rib eye)
1 yellow onion (chopped)
¼ cup mushrooms (if desired)
2 tbsp. milk
Salt to taste
Pepper to taste
Cheddar Cheese, for topping (shredded)

Directions

Wash and dice vegetables.
Crack eggs and mix in a bowl with salt and pepper, along with the yellow onions (and mushrooms if desired.)
Pour 2 tbsps. milk to the eggs and whisk.
Spray the waffle maker with oil. Pour 2 tbsps. batter into waffle maker and cook until crispy. Repeat until all batter is used.
Serve with shredded cheese sprinkled on top if desired.

Classics

The Classic

There is nothing wrong with going with an original classic. Now just in a mini version. See how many you can put on one plate.

Prep Time: 5 Minutes
Cook Time: 5 Minutes
Servings: 4

Ingredients

1 cup flour
1 tbsp. sugar
2 tsp. baking powder
¼ tsp. salt
1 egg
1 cup milk
2 1/2 tsp. melted butter

Directions

Pour the flour, baking powder, salt, and sugar into a medium sized bowl.
Mix the remaining ingredients into a smaller bowl,
Stir in the wet ingredients with the dry and make sure they are mixed together.
Spray the waffle maker with oil. Pour 2 tbsps. batter into waffle maker and cook until crispy. Repeat until all batter is used.
Serve with powdered sugar, maple syrup, fresh berries or jam.

Fritaffle

The mixture of frittatas and waffles. Why not get creative and get the most use out of your waffle maker.

Prep Time: 5 Minutes
Cook Time: 137 Minutes
Servings: 4

Ingredients

1 tsp. canola oil
1 large red yellow bell pepper, diced
2 cup roasted potatoes, cubed
2 cups arugula
8 pieces bacon, cut into 1 inch strips
8 large eggs, whisked
½ Parmesan cheese
1 cup Mozzarella

Directions

Pour the canola oil into a nonstick oven safe pan on medium high. Throw in red peppers. Cook until soft and then add potatoes and cook until warm.

Next, add the arugula and bacon and combine all the ingredients together.

In a medium size bowl, stir in the eggs, salt, pepper, and Parmesan cheese.

Pour the mixture into the pan and make sure it is even on all sides. Stir in ¾ cup of Mozzarella cheese and sprinkle the rest on top.

Cook for 2 minutes until a crust forms on the edge and then move to the oven and bake at 375 degrees for 10 minutes.

Remove from oven and put in fridge for 2 hours.

Stamp out rounds the size of the waffle iron.

Spray the waffle maker with oil. Put a round in the waffle iron until warmed through and crispy. Continue until all of the frittata has been warmed up.

Crinkled Hash Browns

Are these fries or hash browns? Enjoy these crinkled hash brown during any meal.

Prep Time: 5 Minutes
Cook Time: 5 Minutes
Servings: 4

Ingredients

2 medium potatoes, peeled and shredded
½ yellow onion, finely diced
1 egg
2 tbsp. flour
½ tsp. onion powder
½ tsp. salt
¼ tsp. pepper

Directions

Mix all ingredients in a large bowl.
Scoop out small amounts of the mixture into balls and make into patties
Spray the waffle maker with oil. Cook patties one at a time until crisp.
Serve with shredded cheese, salsa or as a side disk to eggs.

Crinkled Cheesy Jalapeño Hash Browns

Are these fries or hash browns? Enjoy these crinkled hash brown during any meal.

Prep Time: 5 Minutes
Cook Time: 5 Minutes
Servings: 4

Ingredients

2 medium potatoes, peeled and shredded
½ yellow onion, finely diced
1 cup cheddar cheese (shredded)
1 Jalapeño (diced)
1 egg
2 tbsp. flour
½ tsp. onion powder
½ tsp. salt
¼ tsp. pepper

Directions

Mix all ingredients in a large bowl.
Scoop out small amounts of the mixture into balls and make into patties
Spray the waffle maker with oil. Cook patties one at a time until crisp.
Serve with additional shredded cheese, salsa or as a side disk to eggs.

The Cinnamon Whipped Cream Double Stack

You can never go wrong when getting ready to indulge in some whipped cream. This little staple is a good one indeed. Simple and crisp but so delicious. Enjoy!

Prep Time: 5 Minutes
Cook Time: 5 Minutes
Servings: 4

Ingredients

1 cup flour
1 tbsp. sugar
2 tsp. baking powder
¼ tsp. salt
1 egg
1 cup milk
2 1/2 tsp. melted butter
1 can whipped cream spray (dairy free is good as well)

Directions

Pour the flour, baking powder, salt, cinnamon and sugar into a medium sized bowl.
Mix the remaining ingredients into a smaller bowl,
Stir in the wet ingredients with the dry and make sure they are mixed together.
Spray the waffle maker with oil. Pour 2 tbsps. batter into waffle maker and cook until crispy. Repeat until all batter is used.
Lay 1 waffle flat and cover with whipped cream.
Put the second waffle on top of the whipped cream, and repeat.

Cinnamon Chocolate Waffle Delight

If you like sweet, then this is the recipe for you. Chocolate, cinnamon and icing. This could be a treat for breakfast or dessert.

Prep Time: 5 Minutes
Cook Time: 5 Minutes
Servings: 1

Ingredients

¾ cup all-purpose flour
2 tbsp. sugar
¼ cup unsweetened cocoa powder
2 tbsp. melted butter
1 cup buttermilk
½ tsp. baking powder
¼ tsp. baking soda
1 large egg
½ cup chocolate chips
1 ¼ tsp. cinnamon
½ tsp. vanilla extract

Cream Cheese Icing
2 tbsp. melted butter
2 tbsp. cream cheese, softened
½ cup powdered sugar
¼ tsp. vanilla extract
2-3 tbsp. milk

Directions

Add the flour, sugar, cocoa powder, cinnamon, vanilla extract, baking powder and baking soda to a medium bowl
Stir the egg, butter, and buttermilk in a separate

bowl. Then mix the wet ingredients with the dry and gently fold in the chocolate chips.

Spray the waffle maker with oil. Pour 2 tbsps. batter into waffle maker and cook until crispy. Repeat until all batter is used.

In a medium bowl, mix the butter and cream cheese until combined. Then stir in the powdered sugar, milk and vanilla extract.

Drizzle the icing over the waffles and serve warm.

Beef:

Texan Taco

Try this recipe on your next taco Tuesday. The warm cornbread waffle paired with the ground beef and other toppings for an ultimate meal.

Prep Time: 15 Minutes
Cook Time: 10 Minutes
Servings: 4

Ingredients

Cornbread waffle
1 ½ cups buttermilk
4 tbsp. melted butter
2 eggs, lightly beaten
1 cup yellow cornmeal
2 tbsp. sugar
2 tbsp. baking soda
2 tbsp. taco seasoning (from package)
1 tsp. salt

Topping
1 lb. ground beef
2/4 cup water
Remaining taco seasoning
1 can diced green chiles
Toppings: chopped lettuce, tomatoes, onions, avocados, shredded cheese, cilantro, and sour cream

Directions

Combine the buttermilk and butter in a bowl and then stir in the eggs.

In another large bowl, mix in the flour, cornmeal, sugar, baking soda, taco seasoning and salt.

Make a well in the center and pour in the buttermilk mixture and mix until combined.

Spray the waffle maker with oil. Pour 2 tbsps. batter into waffle maker and cook until crispy. Repeat until all batter is used.

Heat a large skillet on medium high and cook the ground beef until browned for 7 minutes.

Stir in the water and taco seasoning and heat until boiling.

Reduce the heat and cook until it thickens for 4 minutes. Then stir in the green chiles.

Serve the meat and desired toppings on top of the waffle.

Waffle Burger with Cheese

The thin patty fits exactly in the waffle iron and pairs great with a waffle bun to go with it.

Prep Time: 5 Minutes
Cook Time: 5 Minutes
Servings: 1

Ingredients

Waffle Bun
4 ½ cups unbleached flour
1 ½ tsps. salt
3 tbsps. sugar
2 tsps. Instant yeast
1 egg, lightly beaten
¼ cup butter
1 ½ cup buttermilk

Waffleburger
1 lb. ground beef
Salt to taste
Pepper to taste
Cheese slices

Directions

Add the flour, salt, sugar and yeast in a large bowl. Pour in the egg, gutter and buttermilk and mix together until the dough forms.
Sprinkle the counter with flour and knead the dough for eight minutes.
Transfer the dough to a lightly oiled bowl and cover.
Let rise for two hours.
Removed the dough and divide into 12 pieces. Shape into tight rounds.

Let rise for 90 minutes covered with plastic wrap.
Spray the waffle maker with oil. Place the dough in the mini waffle and close the lid. Cook for 5 minutes until golden brown.
Set aside. Season the beef and form into a thin patty.
Cook on the mini waffle iron for four minutes and top with cheese.
Cook for five seconds Serve with condiments that you desire.

Spaghetti and Zucchi Waffles with Meatballs

Bet you never though that you could have spaghetti in a waffle. Well, now you can, and you're gonna love it.

Prep Time: 5 Minutes
Cook Time: 5 Minutes
Servings: 2

Ingredients

Waffles
1 zucchini, spiral
¾ cup flour
1 egg
1 tbsp. oil
Salt to taste

Meatballs
1 lb. ground beef
1 tsp. smoked paprika
½ tsp. pumpkin spice
1 tbsp. concentrated tomato paste
1 small onion, diced
¾ cup bread crumbs
1 egg

Tomato Sauce
3 tomatoes, diced
1 large onion, diced
1 garlic clove, minced
1 can cherry tomatoes
2 tbsp. tomato paste
1 tbsp. balsamic vinegar

Fresh parsley

Directions

Mix all the meatball ingredients together.

Roll small little balls and pour some olive oil in a frying pan.

Grill the balls until they brown and crisp, about 5-7 minutes.

Add the onion and fry for 2 minutes, and then add the tomatoes, tomato paste, and balsamic vinegar. Put the lid on and cook on low for 15 minutes.

Mix all the waffle ingredients together until combined.

Spray the waffle maker with oil. Pour ¼ cup of the batter into the mini maker waffle and cook until golden brown. Repeat with the remaining batter.

Serve the waffle with a good amount of meatballs and sauce. Top with parsley, mozzarella and Parmesan cheese. Enjoy.

Waffle Seared Filet Mignon

Served with the perfect sear on the outside and perfectly pink on the inside.

Prep Time: 2 Minutes
Cook Time: 8 Minutes
Servings: 2

Ingredients

 2 tsp. salt
2 tsp. pepper
8 oz. filet mignon, cut in half
Nonstick cooking spray

Directions

Pour salt and pepper on a plate & coat the steak with it on both sides.

Spray the waffle maker with the nonstick spray. Place the steak as far away from the hinge as possible. Close the lid and cook for 8 minutes.

Remove the steak and place it on the cutting board. Allow it to rest for several minutes while you put the other piece on and repeat the process.

Serve the steak with mashed potatoes and veggies.

Big Pastromi Waffle Club with Bacon & Kraut

Ok...now we're just getting started. There's so much flavor in this extraordinary waffle sandwich you're going to have to see it for yourself!

Prep Time: 5 Minutes
Cook Time: 5 Minutes
Servings: 1

Ingredients

Waffle Bun
4 ½ cups unbleached flour
1 ½ tsps. salt
3 tbsps. sugar
2 tsps. Instant yeast
1 egg, lightly beaten
¼ cup butter
1 ½ cup buttermilk

Pastromi
1 lb. pastrami
6 strips of cooked bacon (extra crispy)
Salt to taste
Pepper to taste
Parmesan cheese shaved

Directions

Add the flour, salt, sugar and yeast in a large bowl. Pour in the egg, gutter and buttermilk and mix together until the dough forms. Sprinkle the counter with flour and knead the dough for eight minutes.

Transfer the dough to a lightly oiled bowl and cover.

Let rise for two hours.

Removed the dough and divide into 12 pieces. Shape into tight rounds.

Let rise for 90 minutes covered with plastic wrap.

Spray the waffle maker with oil. Place the dough in the mini waffle and close the lid. Cook for 5 minutes until golden brown.

Set aside 3 waffles for each club sandwich.

Cook the pastrami on the mini waffle iron for about 30 secs.to 1 minute. When done top with cheese. Cook for five seconds

Lay down 1 waffle, add 3 strips of bacon then add pastrami and cheese.

Lay down a 2nd waffle on top of the cheese and repeat steps 1.

Serve with condiments that you desire.

Sides:

Crunchy Macaroni and Cheese Waffles

This can be the perfect side dish to any meal. Or you can enjoy all of this cheesy gooiness on its own.

Prep Time: 2 Minutes
Cook Time: 12 Minutes
Servings: 10

Ingredients

1 box macaroni and cheese
2 tbsp. butter
¼ cup milk
1 ½ cup shredded cheddar cheese
1 egg, beaten
1/3 cup bread crumbs
Nonstick cooking spray

Directions

Cook the macaroni and cheese according to the box directions
Spray the waffle maker with cooking spray.
Scoop ¼ cup of the macaroni and cheese into the center of the mini waffle maker and sprinkle with more cheese
Close the lid and cook for 5 minutes until golden and crispy. Repeat until all of the macaroni and cheese is gone.
Serve warm.

Grilled Waffle with Cheese

We all love grilled cheese, but grilled cheese waffles take the cake.

Prep Time: 5 Minutes
Cook Time: 5 Minutes
Servings: 2

Ingredients

2 slices sandwich bread, cut in half
2 cheddar cheese slices, cut in half
2 tbsp. salted butter

Directions

Spread one slice of bread with butter and repeat with all four pieces. Only put butter on one side.
Place the cheese slices on slice of bread at a time. Make sure it is on the side without the butter.
Place one of the pieces on top of the cheese, butter side up and place it down on the mini waffle iron.
Close the top, but do not smash the sandwich
Cook for 5 minutes until the bread is brown and the cheese has melted. Repeat with the other half sandwich.
Serve with a bowl of tomato soup.

Olive Grilled Cheese Waffle

We all love grilled cheese, but grilled cheese waffles take the cake.

Prep Time: 5 Minutes
Cook Time: 5 Minutes
Servings: 2

Ingredients

2 slices sandwich bread, cut in half
2 cheddar cheese slices, cut in half
2 tbsp. salted butter
¼ cup black olives (sliced)

Ranch to dip

Directions

Spread one slice of bread with butter and repeat with all four pieces. Only put butter on one side.
Sprinkle the olives then place the cheese slices one slice of bread at a time. Make sure it is on the side without the butter.
Place one of the pieces on top of the cheese, butter side up and place it down on the mini waffle iron.
Close the top, but do not smash the sandwich
Cook for 5 minutes until the bread is brown and the cheese has melted. Repeat with the other half sandwich.
Serve with Ranch to dip.

Grilled Jalapeño Waffle Club with Cheese

Nice and cheesy this one we have here for you. Nothing says Grilled Cheese than something delicious with maple bacon, jalapeños and cheese! I never knew it could get this good.

Prep Time: 5 Minutes
Cook Time: 5 Minutes
Servings: 2

Ingredients

2 slices sandwich bread, cut in half
2 cheddar cheese slices, cut in half
2 tbsp. salted butter
6 strips of bacon
1 jalapeño diced

Directions

Spread one slice of bread with butter and repeat with all four pieces. Only put butter on one side.
Place the cheese slices on slice of bread at a time. Make sure it is on the side without the butter.
Place one of the pieces on top of the cheese, butter side up and place it down on the mini waffle iron.
Close the top, but do not smash the sandwich
Cook for 5 minutes until the bread is brown and the cheese has melted. Repeat with the other half sandwich to make a triple decker. (3 waffles per sandwich)
Serve with a bowl of tomato soup.

What to Do with My Leftover Mashed Potato Waffles?

Tired of the same old leftovers. Well now you can make your mashed potatoes crispy like a waffle too.

Prep Time: 10 Minutes
Cook Time: 5 Minutes
Servings: 3

Ingredients

2 tbsp. vegetable oil
¼ cup buttermilk
2 large eggs
2 ½ cups leftover mashed potatoes
3 tbsps. scallions, chopped
1 cup cheddar cheese, shredded
½ cup all-purpose flour
½ tsp. baking powder
¼ cup baking soda
Sour cream, for serving

Directions

Stir together oil, buttermilk, and eggs in a large bowl. Add in the mashed potatoes, scallions and cheese until mixed thoroughly.
In a small bowl, mix together the flour, baking powder and baking soda. Fold the flour mixture into the potato mixture.
Spray the waffle maker with oil. Scoop ¼ cup of the potato mixture into the mini maker waffle and cook until golden brown. Repeat with the remaining potato mixture.
Serve the waffle with sour cream and additional scallions.

Mozzarella Waffle Stick

All that cheesy gooiness in that waffle crisp that you love. Let this one take you to heaven and back as you indulge in these mouth-watering waffles.

Prep Time: 30 Minutes
Cook Time: 8 Minutes
Servings: 8

Ingredients

1 cup all-purpose flour
2 large eggs, lightly beaten
2 tbsp. milk
1 cup Italian breadcrumbs
16 mozzarella sticks
Salt to taste
Fresh parsley, chopped for garnish
Marinara, warmed for serving

Directions

Add flour to shallow bowl. Whisk eggs in another shallow bowl and add bread crumbs to a third.
Toss mozzarella sticks in flour, then egg mixture and then bread crumbs.
Spray the waffle maker with oil. Place mozzarella sticks side by side in the waffle iron, 8 at a time. Cover and cook for 4 minutes until golden brown. Repeat.
Serve the waffle with parsley and dip in marinara sauce

The Avacado Tomato Classic

We're mixing up the flavors again to give you something you may have never tasted before. This selection goes well with tomato soup and saltine crackers.

Prep Time: 5 Minutes
Cook Time: 5 Minutes
Servings: 4

Ingredients

1 cup flour
1 tbsp. sugar
2 tsp. baking powder
1 avocado sliced to lay on waffles
1 large tomato cut into sliced circles
¼ tsp. salt
1 egg
1 cup milk
2 1/2 tsp. melted butter

Directions

Pour the flour, baking powder, salt, and sugar into a medium sized bowl.
Mix the butter, milk and eggs into a smaller bowl,
Stir in the wet ingredients with the dry and make sure they are mixed together.
Spray the waffle maker with oil. Pour 2 tbsps. batter into waffle maker and cook until crispy. Lay the avocado slices over one the waffles and top with the tomato. Repeat until all batter is used.
Serve with powdered sugar, maple syrup, fresh berries or jam.

Note: Goes well with tomato soup and saltine crackers.

Pork:

Pepperoni Pizza Waffles

Pizza bagels are out, and pepperoni stuffed waffles are in.

Prep Time: 15 Minutes
Cook Time: 10 Minutes
Servings: 4

Ingredients

1 can refrigerated biscuits
2 cups mozzarella, shredded
¼ cup pizza sauce
1 cup sliced mini pepperoni
Parmesan, grated

Directions

Roll out biscuits into flat patties.
Top half of biscuits with ½ cup of mozzarella and 1 tbsp. of pizza sauce, then add pepperoni. Top with the second biscuit and seal edged
Spray the waffle maker with oil. Place one pizza at a time and cook for 3 minutes. Repeat until all are cooked
Sprinkle parmesan cheese on top and cut into wedges.

Mega Pepperoni Heat Pizza Waffles

This is the DOUBLE DOSE of pepperoni stuffed waffles. A BIGGER and BOLDER way to look at pizza waffles!

Prep Time: 15 Minutes
Cook Time: 10 Minutes
Servings: 4

Ingredients

1 can refrigerated biscuits
2 cups mozzarella, shredded
¼ cup pizza sauce
2 cup sliced mini pepperoni
1 jalapeño diced
Parmesan, grated

Directions

Roll out biscuits into flat patties.
Top half of biscuits with ½ cup of mozzarella and 1 tbsp. of pizza sauce, then add pepperoni. Top with the second biscuit and seal edged
Spray the waffle maker with oil. Place one pizza at a time and cook for 3 minutes. Repeat until all are cooked.
Double the pepperoni for a BIG BOLD FLAVOR!
Sprinkle parmesan cheese on top and cut into wedges.

Basil Sausage & Bacon Waffle Pizza

Pizza bagels are out, and pepperoni stuffed waffles are in.
Prep Time: 15 Minutes
Cook Time: 10 Minutes
Servings: 4

Ingredients

1 can refrigerated biscuits
2 cups mozzarella, shredded
¼ cup pizza sauce
1 tablespoon basil (chopped fine)
1/2 cup cooked ground sausage
1/2 cup cooked bacon
Parmesan, grated

Directions

Roll out biscuits into flat patties.
Top half of biscuits with ½ cup of mozzarella and 1 tbsp of pizza sauce, then add the sausage, basil and bacon. Top with the second biscuit and seal edged
Spray the waffle maker with oil. Place one pizza at a time and cook for 3 minutes. Repeat until all are cooked
Sprinkle parmesan cheese on top and cut into wedges.
Note: If you like it extra gooey then add more cheese!

Bacon Cilantro Artichoke Waffle Pizza

Pizza bagels are out, and pepperoni stuffed waffles are in.
Prep Time: 15 Minutes
Cook Time: 10 Minutes
Servings: 4

Ingredients

1 can refrigerated biscuits
2 cups mozzarella, shredded
¼ cup pizza sauce
1 tablespoon cilantro
1/2 cup artichoke hearts
1/2 cup cooked bacon
Parmesan, grated

Directions

Roll out biscuits into flat patties.
Top half of biscuits with ½ cup of mozzarella and 1 tbsp. of pizza sauce, then add the artichoke, cilantro and bacon. Top with the second biscuit and seal edged
Spray the waffle maker with oil. Place one pizza at a time and cook for 3 minutes. Repeat until all are cooked
Sprinkle parmesan cheese on top and cut into wedges.
Note: If you like it extra gooey then add more cheese!

Pepperoni, Sausage & Kraut Pizza Waffles

You'll never believe it till you try it! .

Prep Time: 15 Minutes
Cook Time: 10 Minutes
Servings: 4

Ingredients

1 can refrigerated biscuits
2 cups mozzarella, shredded
¼ cup pizza sauce
½ cup sliced mini pepperoni
½ cup cooked ground turkey sausage
Parmesan, grated
½ cup sour kraut

Directions

Roll out biscuits into flat patties.
Top half of biscuits with ½ cup of mozzarella and 1 tbsp. of pizza sauce, then add pepperoni & sausage. Top with the second biscuit and seal edged.
Spray the waffle maker with oil. Place one pizza at a time and cook for 3 minutes. Repeat until all are cooked.
Sprinkle parmesan cheese and lightly spread the kraut on top and cut into wedges.

Corn Dogged Waffle

Another way to eat a hot dog.
Prep Time: 15 Minutes
Cook Time: 5 Minutes
Servings: 2-4

Ingredients

4 hot dogs
1 box corn muffin mix
1 large egg
½ cup sour cream
2 tbsp. melted butter
½ cup cheddar, shredded
2 tbsp. chives
Ketchup and mustard for dipping

Directions

Mix the corn muffin mix, egg and sour cream in a large bowl. Stir until combined.
Toss in the cheddar cheese and chives.
Cut each hot dog in half long ways and then cross wise. Stick a skewer into each piece
Spread ¼ of the batter on the waffle iron. Place the hot dogs on top, and then spread ¼ batter on top.
Close the iron and cook for 4 minutes.
Carefully remove and slice into eighths. Repeat with the rest.
Serve with ketchup and mustard for dipping.

Garlic & Chives Corn Dogged Waffle

Another way to eat a hot dog.
Prep Time: 15 Minutes
Cook Time: 5 Minutes
Servings: 2-4

Ingredients

4 hot dogs
1 box corn muffin mix
1 large egg
½ cup sour cream
2 tbsp. melted butter
½ cup cheddar, shredded
2 tbsp. chives
1 tbsp. garlic

Dippig Sauce:
Ketchup
Mustard
Mayonnaise

Directions

Mix the corn muffin mix, egg and sour cream in a large bowl. Stir until combined.
Toss in the cheddar cheese and chives.
Cut each hot dog in half long ways and then cross wise. Stick a skewer into each piece
Spread ¼ of the batter on the waffle iron. Place the hot dogs on top, and then spread ¼ batter on top.
Close the iron and cook for 4 minutes.
Carefully remove and slice into eighths. Repeat with the rest.
Mix the ketchup, mustard, mayo and pickle relish together

Use the sauce for dipping.

Mini Waffle Maker Cooked Bacon

Bacon cooked with no grease. Sounds like a win to us.
Prep Time: 5 Minutes
Cook Time: 5 Minutes
Servings: 2

Ingredients

8 pieces of bacon, cut in half

Directions

Spray the waffle maker with oil. Place 1 piece on each square of your mini waffle and let cook for 4 minutes. Repeat.
Serve the bacon with eggs or on top of a BLT sandwich.

Spinach Artichoke Garlic Pizza Waffles

Life just keeps getting better! Now we're just showing off. Lol just kidding. Don't knock it till you've tried it. "Dig in!"

Prep Time: 15 Minutes
Cook Time: 10 Minutes
Servings: 4

Ingredients

1 can refrigerated biscuits
2 cups mozzarella, shredded
¼ cup pizza sauce
1 cup sliced mini pepperoni
Parmesan, grated

Directions

Roll out biscuits into flat patties.
Top half of biscuits with ½ cup of mozzarella and 1 tbsp. of pizza sauce, then add pepperoni. Top with the second biscuit and seal edged
Spray the waffle maker with oil. Place one pizza at a time and cook for 3 minutes. Repeat until all are cooked
Sprinkle parmesan cheese on top and cut into wedges.

Poultry:

West Coast Chicken & Waffles

Chicken and waffles just seems so right! This is so good that there are restaurants that specialize in this fancy little "southern" dish. Enjoy!.

Prep Time: 5 Minutes
Cook Time: 5 Minutes
Servings: 2

Ingredients

Chicken:
1 chicken breast, pounded to an even thickness
2 cups. buttermilk
2 cups all-purpose flour
2 ¼ tsp. Kosher salt
1 tsp. cayenne
1 tbsp. garlic powder
Vegetable oil, for frying

Waffles:
1 cup flour
1 tbsp. sugar
2 tsp. baking powder
¼ tsp. salt
1 egg
1 cup milk
2 1/2 tsp. melted butter
spray oil for waffle maker

Directions

Chicken: After letting the chicken soak in buttermilk for at least 12hrs, take out and set to the side.

Combine 1 cup of flour with 2 tsp. salt, garlic powder and cayenne pepper. Coat the chicken in the flour mixture with a nice coat. Dip the chicken into the buttermilk again, then into the flour for a second time. This should make it nice and crispy. The oil needs to be heated to 350 degrees F and Fry chicken for 6 to 8 minutes. Use a cooking thermometer to achieve a temperature of 165 degrees F. Drain on paper towel and Set aside.

Waffle: Pour flour, baking powder, salt, & sugar into a medium sized bowl.
Mix the remaining ingredients into a smaller bowl,
Stir in the wet ingredients with the dry and make sure they are mixed together.
Spray the waffle maker with oil. Pour 2 tbsps. batter into waffle maker and cook until crispy. Repeat until all batter is used.
Serve with powdered sugar, maple syrup, fresh berries or jam. Delicious!!!

Cheesy Chicken Quesadilla Waffles

Bet you never though that you could have spaghetti in a waffle. Well, now you can, and you're gonna love it.

Prep Time: 5 Minutes
Cook Time: 5 Minutes
Servings: 2

Ingredients

2 chicken breasts, cooked and shredded
2 flour tortillas
1 cup mozzarella cheese, shredded
Cooking spray

Directions

Spray the waffle maker with the cooking spray.
Place one small tortilla on the bottom of the waffle maker and stack with chicken, and cheese.
Place the other tortilla on top.
Cook for 4 minutes until cheese is gooey.
Serve the quesadilla with sour cream and salsa.

Nacho Chicken and Waffles

Another twist on a classic… Now you can have you sweet, savory and Mexican all at once. Make this a regular Tuesday or Thursday night.

Prep Time: 5 Minutes
Cook Time: 15 Minutes
Servings: 6-8

Ingredients

Waffles
2 ½ cups all-purpose flour
2 tsp. baking powder
1 ½ tsp. salt
2 eggs
1 egg yolk
2 cup milk
10 tbsp. unsalted butter melted
1 ½ cups cheddar cheese
½ cup Parmesan cheese

Cheese sauce
2 tbsp. butter
1 tbsp. flour
1 cup milk
1 ½ cups cheddar cheese

7 slices bacon, cooked
3 cups popcorn chicken
2 tbsp. Sriracha
2 tbsp. scallions

Directions

Waffles: Stir flour, baking powder and salt into a large bowl.
Mix the eggs and egg yolk in a small bowl until yolks are broken.
Pour in the milk and butter while whisking the eggs.
Pour the egg mixture into the flour mixture and mix well.
Spray the waffle maker with oil. Pour ¼ cup of the batter into the
mini maker waffle and cook until golden brown. Repeat with the
remaining batter.
Cheese sauce: Add butter to a medium skillet over medium heat.
Cook for 3 minutes.
Stir in flour and cook for 3 minutes. Pour in milk and turn up heat to
medium high.
Toss in cheese and cook until melted.
Take the pan off of the burner, and stir until cheese is completely
melted, thick and combined
Assemble: Cut the waffles into quarters and cover bottom of plate.
Pour 2/4 of cheese sauce on top and then add bacon and popcorn
chicken. Drizzle more cheese on top of chicken with Sriracha and
scallions.
Serve immediately.

Fish:

Crab Cake Waffle Style

Another way to enjoy this delicious fish dish. You can serve it on a bun or eat it by itself.

Prep Time: 5 Minutes
Cook Time: 30 Minutes
Servings: 2

Ingredients

9 oz. lump crab meat
½ cup breadcrumbs
1 large egg, beaten
1 large egg white
1 tbsp. mayonnaise
1 tbsp. Dijon mustard
2 tbsp. chives, chopped
2 tbsp. fresh parsley, minced
1 tbsp. fresh lemon juice
½ tsp. Old Bay Seasoning
1/8 tsp. paprika
Tobacco, to taste
Salt, to taste
Pepper, to taste
4 lemon wedges, for serving
Cooking spray

Directions

Mix the breadcrumbs, egg, mayonnaise, Dijon mustard, chives, parsley, lemon juice, Old Bay Seasoning, paprika, tabasco, salt and pepper together in a large bowl. Then add in the crab meat and mix well.

Shape into think, flattened patties. Makes about four

Spray the waffle maker with oil. Place one in the center and close the lid gently.
Cook for 3 minutes until golden brown.
Serve with lemon wedges.

Shrimp Style Crab Cake Waffle Style

Another way to enjoy this delicious fish dish. You can serve it on a bun or eat it by itself.

Prep Time: 5 Minutes
Cook Time: 30 Minutes
Servings: 2

Ingredients

10 oz. shrimp meat chopped
½ cup breadcrumbs
1 large egg, beaten
1 large egg white
1 tbsp. mayonnaise
1 tbsp. Dijon mustard
2 tbsp. chives, chopped
2 tbsp. fresh parsley, minced
1 tbsp. fresh lemon juice
½ tsp. Old Bay Seasoning
1/8 tsp. paprika
Tobacco, to taste
Salt, to taste
Pepper, to taste
4 lemon wedges, for serving
Cooking spray

Directions

Mix the breadcrumbs, egg, mayonnaise, Dijon mustard, chives, parsley, lemon juice, Old Bay Seasoning, paprika, tabasco, salt and pepper together in a large bowl. Then add in the well chopped up shrimp and mix well.
Shape into think, flattened patties. Makes about four.

Spray the waffle maker with oil. Place one in the center and close the lid gently.
Cook for 3 minutes until golden brown.
Serve with lemon wedges.

Tuna Cakes Waffle Style

Another way to enjoy this delicious fish dish. You can serve it on a bun or eat it by itself.

Prep Time: 5 Minutes
Cook Time: 30 Minutes
Servings: 2

Ingredients

9 oz. tuna (in water if canned)
½ cup breadcrumbs
1 large egg, beaten
1 large egg white
1 tbsp. mayonnaise
1 tbsp. Dijon mustard
2 tbsp. chives, chopped
2 tbsp. fresh parsley, minced
1 tbsp. fresh lemon juice
½ tsp. Old Bay Seasoning
1/8 tsp. paprika
Tobacco, to taste
Salt, to taste
Pepper, to taste
4 lemon wedges, for serving
Cooking spray

Directions

Mix the breadcrumbs, egg, mayonnaise, Dijon mustard, chives, parsley, lemon juice, Old Bay Seasoning, paprika, tabasco, salt and pepper together in a large bowl. Then add in the well chopped up tuna and mix well.

Shape into think, flattened patties. Makes about four

Spray the waffle maker with oil. Place one in the center and close the lid gently.
Cook for 3 minutes until golden brown.
Serve with lemon wedges.

The Lumped Crab Waffle

Seafood is on the menu! Come and get it while it's hot! This is one of our favorites for you to enjoy! Put this recipe next on your list and you will be a true believer! Enjoy!

Prep Time: 5 Minutes
Cook Time: 5 Minutes
Servings: 4

Ingredients

9 oz. lump crab meat
1 cup flour
1 tbsp. sugar
2 tsp. baking powder
¼ tsp. salt
1 egg
1 cup milk
½ cup green onions
2 1/2 tsp. melted butter

Directions

Pour the flour, baking powder, salt, and sugar into a medium sized bowl.
Mix the remaining ingredients into a smaller bowl,
Stir in the wet ingredients with the dry and make sure they are mixed together.
Spray the waffle maker with oil. Pour 2 tbsps. batter into waffle maker and cook until crispy. Repeat until all batter is used.

Note: This special treat is best served with just a sprinkle of powdered sugar on each piece. Then dip in butter (grass fed).

The Jumbo Shrimp Waffle

This seafood lover's dream is special on our menu as well. This is something you may want to spice up with a little cocktail sauce at the end! Enjoy!

Prep Time: 5 Minutes
Cook Time: 5 Minutes
Servings: 4

Ingredients

9 oz. shrimp (chopped up fine)
1 cup flour
1 tbsp. sugar
2 tsp. baking powder
¼ tsp. salt
1 egg
1 cup milk
½ cup green onions
2 1/2 tsp. melted butter

Directions

Heat a non-stick pan on medium heat. Cook the shrimp for about 2 minutes on high until it lightly starts to brown and set aside.
Pour the flour, baking powder, salt, and sugar into a medium sized bowl.
Mix the remaining ingredients into a smaller bowl,
Stir in the wet ingredients with the dry and make sure they are mixed together. Add the shrimp to the mixture and mix 1 last time.
Spray the waffle maker with oil. Pour 2 tbsps. batter into waffle maker and cook until crispy. Repeat until all batter is used.

Note: This special treat is best served with cocktail sauce.

The Succulent Scallops Waffle

Scallops when cooked correctly, will give you a melt in your mouth seafood flavor that you just don't get every day! This one is fun and enjoyable and we hope you love it!

Prep Time: 5 Minutes
Cook Time: 5 Minutes
Servings: 4

Ingredients

9 oz. scallops
1 cup flour
1 tbsp. sugar
2 tsp. baking powder
¼ tsp. salt
1 egg
1 cup milk
½ cup green onions
2 1/2 tsp. melted butter

Directions

Heat a non-stick pan on medium heat. Cook the scallops for about 1 to 1 and ½ minutes on high until it lightly starts to brown. Flip, repeat on the second side. When done set aside.
Pour the flour, baking powder, salt, and sugar into a medium sized bowl.
Mix the remaining ingredients into a smaller bowl,
Stir in the wet ingredients with the dry and make sure they are mixed together. Cut up the scallops very fine and add to the mixture and mix 1 last time.
Spray the waffle maker with oil. Pour 2 tbsps. batter into waffle maker and cook until crispy. Repeat until all batter is used.

Note: Served best with a lemon butter sauce to dip.

Miso Glazed Waffled Salmon

Bet you never though that you could have spaghetti in a waffle. Well, now you can, and you're gonna love it.

Prep Time: 5 Minutes
Cook Time: 8 Minutes
Servings: 2

Ingredients
1 tbsp. maple syrup
2 tsp. yellow miso paste
1 tsp. distilled white vinegar
1 tsp. pure sesame oil
½ tsp. fresh ginger, grated
1 garlic clove, minced
2 salmon fillets, 4-6 oz. each
8 oz. asparagus, washed with bottoms removed
¼ cup extra-virgin olive oil
Salt, to taste
Pepper, to taste
Nonstick cooking spray

Directions
Mix the maple syrup, miso, vinegar, sesame oil, ginger and garlic in a small bowl. Set aside.
Spray the waffle maker with cooking spray. Place the salmon, skin side down, on the mini waffle maker (one at a time) and close the lid.
Toss the asparagus with the olive oil, and salt and pepper in another bowl.
Check the fish after 4 minutes.

Baste the salmon with the glaze, close the lid, and cook for 1 more minute.
Remove the fish and add the other piece and repeat the process.
Place the asparagus in the mini waffle maker and close the lid and cook for 3 minutes.
Serve along with the salmon.

Dessert:

Waffle Ice Cream Sandwiches

A great recipe for the kids to make at home during the summer. Now they won't want to go out for ice cream anymore.

Prep Time: 40 Minutes
Cook Time: 10 Minutes
Servings: 2

Ingredients

Waffles
1 cup flour
1 tbsp. sugar
2 tsp. baking powder
¼ tsp. salt
1 egg
1 cup milk
2 1/2 tsp. melted butter

2 cups ice cream
Ice cream toppings

Directions

Pour the flour, baking powder, salt, and sugar into a medium sized bowl.
Mix the remaining ingredients into a smaller bowl,
Stir in the wet ingredients with the dry and make sure they are mixed together.
Spray the waffle maker with oil. Pour 2 tbsps. batter into waffle maker and cook until crispy. Repeat until all batter is used.
Place the waffles in freezer until hard.
Top with ice cream and other toppings. Place the second waffle on top.
Clean up the edges.

Place into freezer until hard.
Slice into quarters.
Serve and enjoy.

Waffle Snickerdoodles

Cookies in the shape of waffles. They will have a crunchy, but light consistency that will blow you away.

Prep Time: 10 Minutes
Cook Time: 10 Minutes
Servings: 2 dozen

Ingredients
½ cup butter, softened
½ cup granulated sugar
¼ cup brown sugar, packed
1 large egg
1 tsp. vanilla
1 ¼ cup all-purpose flour
¼ tsp. baking soda
¼ tsp. cinnamon
¼ tsp salt
2 oz. cream cheese, softened
1/3 cup powdered sugar
½ tsp. vanilla
Milk, for glaze consistency

Directions
Whisk the butter and sugars together until light and fluffy. Sir in egg and vanilla. Slowly pour in dry ingredients.
Spray the waffle maker with cooking spray. Scoop cookie dough into small forms and place on the mini waffle maker.
Close the waffle iron and cook for 2 minutes.
Remove and let cool.
Glaze: mix the sugar, vanilla and cream cheese together until smooth. Slowly stir in the milk.

Drizzle over the cookies and top with more cinnamon.
Serve and enjoy.

Waffle Brownie A La Mode

What better than a brownie waffle? The sweet and crispiness will melt in your mouth.

Prep Time: 5 Minutes
Cook Time: 10 Minutes
Servings: 3

Ingredients

1 ½ cup all-purpose flour
½ cup unsweetened cocoa powder
1 cup granulated sugar
1 tsp. baking powder
1 tsp. sea salt
10 tsp. unsalted butter, melted
2 large eggs
2 tsp. vanilla extract
¼ cup water
2/3 cups mini chocolate chips
Optional toppings: vanilla ice cream, chocolate sauce, powdered sugar

Directions

Pour the flour, cocoa powder, sugar, baking powder, and salt in a large bowl.
Melt the butter and set aside.
Whisk the eggs, vanilla extract, and water in a small bowl. Mix the egg mixture into the dry mixture.
Quickly add the butter and stir in the chocolate chips.
Spray the waffle maker with cooking spray. Pour ¼ of the batter into the mini waffle maker, close the lid and cook for 3 minutes.
Take it out to crisp up.

Repeat with the remaining batter.
Serve as is or with powdered sugar, or a la mode with vanilla ice cream and chocolate sauce.

Waffle Cupcakes

Who needs cake when you have waffle batter instead? The kids will be begging for these from now on.

Prep Time: 10 Minutes
Cook Time: 10 Minutes
Servings: 2

Ingredients

1 box cake mix,

Directions

Mix the ingredients for the cake mix according to the package
Spray the waffle maker with cooking spray. Pour ¼ of the cake mix in the mini waffle maker and close the lid.
Cook for no more than 3 minutes.
Separate into sections and let cool.
Place the waffles in freezer until hard.

Note:
Place the waffle on the plate and scoop some ice cream on the top if desired. Sandwich two pieces of waffle between the ice cream.
Serve and enjoy.

Blueberry Cinnamon Waffle Cupcakes

Blueberry will be the best thing on the block when you get hold of this special delight. The flavors in this dish will make you fall in love with it! Enjoy!.

Prep Time: 15 Minutes
Cook Time: 10 Minutes
Servings: 2

Ingredients

1 box cake mix,
1 container butter cream frosting
1 cup blueberries (mashed)
1 teaspoon cinnamon
1 teaspoon vanilla

Directions

Mix the ingredients for the cake mix according to the package and add the mashed blueberries and cinnamon and vanilla.
Spray the waffle maker with cooking spray. Pour ¼ of the cake mix in the mini waffle maker and close the lid.
Cook for no more than 3 minutes.
Separate into sections and let cool.
Spread on the butter cream icing to each of the waffle pieces and enjoy.

Waffle Mini Donuts

Amazing cake donuts made in the waffle maker and drizzled with a cinnamon sugar coating.

Prep Time: 5 Minutes
Cook Time: 10 Minutes
Servings: 16

Ingredients
1 cup sugar
4 tsp. baking powder
1 ½ tsp salt
½ tsp nutmeg
2 eggs
¼ cup unsalted butter, melted
1 cup milk
3 cups flour

Topping:
2 tsp cinnamon
1 cup white sugar
½ cup butter, melted

Directions
Mix the sugar, baking powder, salt and nutmeg in a large bowl.
Pour the eggs, milk, and melted butter. Beat well.
Next, stir in the 2 cups of flour, mixing well until thoroughly combined
Spray the waffle maker with oil. Pour in the middle of each waffle part to make small doughnuts.
Cook for 3 minutes.
Remove the doughnuts form the waffle maker and place on a cooling rack.
Combine the white sugar and cinnamon for topping.

Dip the waffle in the butter, then shake and dip into the cinnamon mixture.
Serve and enjoy.

Nutmeg Waffle Mini Donuts with Butter Cream Icing

Amazing cake donuts made in the waffle maker and drizzled with a cinnamon sugar coating.

Prep Time: 5 Minutes
Cook Time: 10 Minutes
Servings: 16

Ingredients

1 cup sugar
4 tsp. baking powder
1 ½ tsp salt
½ tsp nutmeg
2 eggs
¼ cup unsalted butter, melted
1 cup milk
3 cups flour

Topping:
1 container of butter cream frosting

Directions

Mix the sugar, baking powder, salt and nutmeg in a large bowl.
Pour the eggs, milk, and melted butter. Beat well.
Next, stir in the 2 cups of flour, mixing well until thoroughly combined
Spray the waffle maker with oil. Pour in the middle of each waffle part to make small doughnuts.
Cook for 3 minutes.
Remove the doughnuts form the waffle maker and place on a cooling rack.
Rub on the frosting with a rubber mallet to top on the topping.

Serve and enjoy.

Pinapple Buttery Basil Waffle Mini Donuts

Amazing cake donuts made in the waffle maker and drizzled with a cinnamon sugar coating.

Prep Time: 5 Minutes
Cook Time: 10 Minutes
Servings: 16

Ingredients

1 cup sugar
½ cup Pineapple
4 tsp. baking powder
1 ½ tsp salt
¼ cup chopped basil
2 eggs
¼ cup unsalted butter, melted
1 cup milk
3 cups flour

Directions

Mix the sugar, baking powder, salt and basil in a large bowl.
Pour the eggs, milk, and melted butter. Beat well.
Next, stir in the 2 cups of flour, mixing well until thoroughly combined
Spray the waffle maker with oil. Pour in the middle of each waffle part to make small doughnuts.
Cook for 3 minutes.
Remove the doughnuts form the waffle maker and place on a cooling rack.
Serve and enjoy.

Note: This enjoyable delight serves well with maple syrup for the topping.

Georgia Peach Heavenly Muffin Waffles

All the savory flavors of Georgia Peach muffins without the wait.

Prep Time: 10 Minutes
Cook Time: 10 Minutes
Servings: 4

Ingredients

1 ½ cups flour
¾ cup sugar
½ tsp. salt
2 tsp. baking powder
1/3 vegetable oil
1 egg
2/3 cup milk
1 cup diced peaches
Butter, melted

Directions

Mix the flour, sugar, salt and baking powder in a bowl. Make a well in the center and add the egg, milk and oil. Stir gently while add the peaches.

Spray the waffle maker with melted butter. Pour ¼ of the batter into the mini waffle maker. Cook for 4 minutes until golden brown. Repeat.

Can be served with whipped cream!

Apple Strawberry Waffle Mini Donuts with Butter Cream Icing

Waffles have never tasted so good! We are combining flavors you may not ever mix. This can always make a big difference in tasting something better.

Prep Time: 5 Minutes
Cook Time: 10 Minutes
Servings: 16

Ingredients

1 cup sugar
4 tsp. baking powder
1 ½ tsp salt
¼ cup apples diced
¼ cup strawberries diced
2 eggs
¼ cup unsalted butter, melted
1 cup milk
3 cups flour

Topping:
1 container of butter cream frosting

Directions

Mix the sugar, baking powder, salt and nutmeg in a large bowl.
Pour the eggs, milk, and melted butter, apples and strawberries.
Beat well.
Next, stir in the 2 cups of flour, mixing well until thoroughly combined
Spray the waffle maker with oil. Pour in the middle of each waffle part to make small doughnuts.
Cook for 3 minutes.

Remove the doughnuts form the waffle maker and place on a cooling rack.
Rub on the frosting with a rubber mallet to top on the topping.
Serve and enjoy.

Vanilla Pumpkin Spice Muffin Waffles

The flavor just keeps on coming! This is a very sweet and pleasant aroma therapy when making these delights. You and your home will be very happy.

Prep Time: 10 Minutes
Cook Time: 10 Minutes
Servings: 4

Ingredients
 1 ½ cups flour
¾ cup sugar
½ tsp. salt
2 tsp. baking powder
1/3 vegetable oil
1 egg
2/3 cup milk
1 tsp. pumpkin spice
½ tsp. vanilla
Butter, melted

Directions
Mix the flour, sugar, salt pumpkin spice and baking powder in a bowl. Make a well in the center and add the egg, milk vanilla and oil. Stir gently while add the blueberries.
Spray the waffle maker with melted butter. Pour ¼ of the batter into the mini waffle maker. Cook for 4 minutes until golden brown. Repeat.
Serve and enjoy.

Kiwi Blackberry Brown Sugar Muffin Waffles

All the deliciousness of blackberry muffins without the wait.

Prep Time: 10 Minutes
Cook Time: 10 Minutes
Servings: 4

Ingredients

1 ½ cups flour
½ cup sugar
¼ cup brown sugar
½ tsp. salt
2 tsp. baking powder
1/3 vegetable oil
1 egg
2/3 cup milk
½ cup kiwi
½ cup blackberries
Butter, melted

Directions

Mix the flour, sugar, brown sugar, salt and baking powder in a bowl. Make a well in the center and add the egg, milk and oil. Stir gently while add the kiwi and blackberries.
Spray the waffle maker with melted butter. Pour ¼ of the batter into the mini waffle maker. Cook for 4 minutes until golden brown. Repeat.
Serve and enjoy.

Printed in Great Britain
by Amazon